Eddie is one of the famous Red Mask Gang of bank robbers. And he's feeling rich after the last bank robbery. He rents one of the beautiful Blue Lake Cabins in the mountains. One day, Eddie goes for a drive. The mountain road is dangerous in the rain.

Suddenly, Eddie's car goes off the road.
'Oh, no!' says Eddie.
But it is too late. He can't stop the car.

Eddie dies. But he leaves behind $3000 from the bank robbery.
Writer Cal Dexter finds it. At first he's excited.
But soon some people come looking for the money. And these people are dangerous . . .

OXFORD BOOKWORMS LIBRARY

Crime & Mystery

Dead Man's Money

Starter (250 headwords)

JOHN ESCOTT

Dead Man's Money

Illustrated by
Dave Hill

OXFORD UNIVERSITY PRESS

OXFORD
UNIVERSITY PRESS

Great Clarendon Street, Oxford OX2 6DP

Oxford University Press is a department of the University of Oxford.
It furthers the University's objective of excellence in research, scholarship,
and education by publishing worldwide in

Oxford New York

Auckland Cape Town Dar es Salaam Hong Kong Karachi
Kuala Lumpur Madrid Melbourne Mexico City Nairobi
New Delhi Shanghai Taipei Toronto

With offices in

Argentina Austria Brazil Chile Czech Republic France Greece
Guatemala Hungary Italy Japan Poland Portugal Singapore
South Korea Switzerland Thailand Turkey Ukraine Vietnam

OXFORD and OXFORD ENGLISH are registered trade marks of
Oxford University Press in the UK and in certain other countries

ISBN: 978 0 19 479365 0

Printed in China
Word count (main text): 1,260

For more information on the Oxford Bookworms Library,
visit www.oup.com/elt/bookworms

CONTENTS

DEAD MAN'S MONEY

The year is 1931. Two men run out of a bank in a little American town. Joe and Eddie are bank robbers. Joe's girlfriend, Blanche, is their driver. She is waiting in the car.

The newspapers call them The Red Mask Gang.

Suddenly, Blanche sees a car.

The police!

They're getting nearer!

Faster, Blanche!

Blanche drives the car faster, but it is dangerous.

It's OK, Blanche! The police car is off the road!

Two hours later, Blanche drives into a town.

You can leave me here. I'm going to rent a car. There are some cabins near here. The Blue Lake Cabins. I can stay there for a week or two.

OK, Eddie. Phone us in two or three weeks. We're going to stay with Blanche's mother.

Eddie takes his share of the money.
He watches Blanche and Joe drive away.

Eddie gets a room for the night. Then he counts his share of the money.

Three thousand dollars!

Next morning, Eddie rents a car.

How far are the Blue Lake Cabins?

Not far. Wilma Pinch usually has cabins to rent.

Half an hour later, Eddie arrives at the Blue Lake Cabins.

I want your best cabin for a week or two.

OK. What's your name?

Er – Collins. Edward Collins.

Where can I put my money?

In a different cabin, a man is working. His name is Cal Dexter, and he is a writer.

Later, Eddie goes and sits by the lake. It is a beautiful morning. Three or four minutes later, Cal comes down to the lake.

Hi, there! How long are you staying?

Hi. A week or two.

I'm here for the summer. You've got a cabin near the lake. They're too expensive for me. Have you got lots of money?

Yes!

That evening, Wilma Pinch sits outside her cabin. She looks at Eddie's cabin.

He's only twenty or twenty-one. But he's got a lot of money.

For the next three days, Eddie is very happy . . .

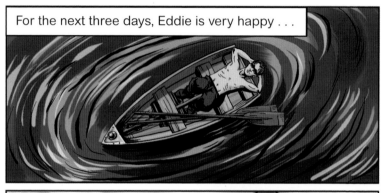

On day four, Eddie goes for a drive.

The next morning, a police car arrives at the Blue Lake Cabins. The policemen tell Wilma about Eddie.

The young man is dead. An accident in the rain. It's a dangerous road.

Bring his things to us later today.

OK.

Wilma tells Cal Dexter about Mr Collins.

That's bad . . .

But can I move into Mr Collins' cabin?

OK, but it's another twenty dollars a week.

That's OK. I got $200 for my story!

Wilma goes to Eddie's cabin. She puts his things in his bag.

Later that day, Wilma gets ready to take Eddie's things to the police.

What's this?

The Red Mask Gang! Mr Collins!

Is some of the bank money in Mr Collins' cabin?

I must find the money before Mr Dexter takes it.

Wilma can't sleep. She goes for a walk by the lake.

Has Dexter got the money?

So Dexter has got the money! What's he going to do with it?

Three thousand dollars! Do I take it to the police? Or tell Wilma Pinch? No, not Wilma. I need to think about this.

It's the money from the bank robbery. But how do I get it?

In a different town, Joe and Blanche are listening to the news. It is about a car accident near the Blue Lake Cabins.

. . . police are trying to find out about the dead man. His name is Edward Collins. He is about twenty years old, tall with red hair . . .

Eddie!

Yes! But what about the money?

Maybe the police don't know where it is.

We must drive up to the Blue Lake Cabins today.

That afternoon, Cal goes out onto the lake.

Now is a good time to look for the money.

The money!

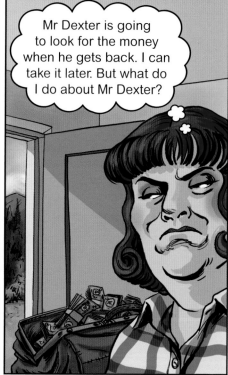

Mr Dexter is going to look for the money when he gets back. I can take it later. But what do I do about Mr Dexter?

Later that day . . .

We want to rent a cabin.

There's one near the lake. It's expensive.

That's OK.

A young man with money! That's interesting.

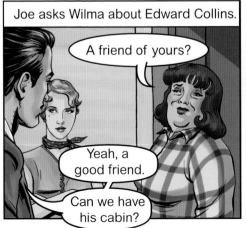

Joe asks Wilma about Edward Collins.

A friend of yours?

Yeah, a good friend.

Can we have his cabin?

Sorry, Mr Dexter's got it now.

Half an hour later, they go down to the lake.

In Cal's cabin, Cal shows Blanche his new story. Joe is thinking about Eddie's share of the money.

Has he got it? It's time to see.

We want the money, Cal. Eddie's money.

Wh – what money? Who is Eddie?

Three thousand dollars. And you're going to give it to us.

OK, OK!

It's all here, Joe.

When Dexter goes into town, there's going to be an accident. Then I can take the money.

It's time for us to go, Cal. Maybe you can write a story about this!

We can be in the town by midnight.

GLOSSARY

accident something bad that happens

bank a building to put your money in

brake the brakes make your car stop

cabin a small house

count *(v)* to see how much of something there is

dangerous something that can hurt or kill you

dollars American money

gang a group of people who do bad things

gas the American word for petrol – you put it in a car to make it go

lake a big area of water

mask something to put over your face, so that people do not know you

maybe perhaps

news when someone tells you or writes about something new

newspaper you can read about things that happen every day in this

outside not in a building

police people who stop other people doing bad things

rent *(v)* to pay money to use something

robber somebody who takes something that is not theirs

share how much one person gets of something

story *Dead Man's Money* is not true; it is a story

thousand one thousand = 1000

Dead Man's Money

ACTIVITIES

ACTIVITIES

Before Reading

1 Look at the front cover of the book and answer these questions.

1 When do you think the story happens?

a ☐ today

b ☐ 1930s

c ☐ 2020

2 Where do you think the story happens?

a ☐ France

b ☐ England

c ☐ America

2 Read the back cover of the book and answer these questions.

1 What does Cal find under the floor of the cabin?

2 Where is it from?

3 Do you think Cal is going to . . .

    a take it to the police?

    b put it back under the floor?

    c lose it?

ACTIVITIES

While Reading

1 Read pages 1–5, then answer these questions.

1 Who are the three people in the Red Mask Gang?
2 Who drives the gang's car?
3 What happens to the police car?
4 Where is Eddie going to stay for a week or two?
5 How much is Eddie's share of the money?

2 Read pages 6–9. Match the words with the pictures.

a 'He's only twenty or twenty-one. But he's got a lot of money.'
b 'Oh, no! No! NO!'
c 'Er – Collins. Edward Collins.'
d 'Where can I put my money?'
e 'Hi, there! How long are you staying?'

3 Read pages 10–15. Are these sentences true (T) or false (F)?

	T	F
1 The police take Eddie's things to the police station.	☐	☐
2 Wilma finds a red mask in Eddie's coat.	☐	☐
3 Wilma finds the money in Cal's cabin.	☐	☐
4 Joe and Blanche hear about Eddie's car accident on the radio.	☐	☐

4 Read pages 16–23 and answer these questions.

Who . . . ?

1 . . . goes out onto the lake?
2 . . . asks Wilma about Edward Collins?
3 . . . knows about car brakes?
4 . . has a gun?

Why . . . ?

5 . . . can't Blanche get their car to start?
6 . . . can't Blanche stop Cal's car?

5 Before you read page 24, can you guess what happens?

	Yes	No
1 Joe and Blanche escape with the money.	☐	☐
2 Wilma gets the money after the car crashes.	☐	☐
3 Wilma and Cal share the money after the car crashes.	☐	☐
4 Nobody gets the money.	☐	☐

ACTIVITIES

After Reading

1 **Complete this summary of some of the story. Use these words:**

newspapers floor Mask money accident wants share robbers

Joe, Blanche, and Eddie are bank _____. The _____ call them The Red _____ Gang. After a robbery, Eddie goes to stay at the Blue Lake Cabins. He puts his _____ of the robbery money under the _____. Eddie dies in a car _____. Cal Dexter finds the _____, but Wilma Pinch sees him. Now she _____ the money, too.

2 **Use these words to join the sentences together.**

but when for and

1 'I can stay there. A week or two.'
2 Blanche drives the car faster. It's dangerous.
3 His name is Cal Dexter. He is a writer.
4 'Dexter is going to look for the money. He gets back.'

3 Look at each picture and answer the questions.

1

Who is this?

2

Where is this car?

3

Who is this? What is she doing?

4

Who is listening to this radio?

5

Who is holding this gun?

6

Who is this?

ABOUT THE AUTHOR

John Escott worked in business before becoming a writer. He has written many books for readers of all ages, but enjoys writing crime and mystery thrillers most of all. He was born in Somerset, in the west of England, but now lives in Bournemouth, on the south coast.

He has written or retold more than twenty stories for the Oxford Bookworms Library. His original stories include *Star Reporter* (Starter), *Girl on a Motorcycle* (Starter), *Goodbye, Mr Hollywood* (Stage 1), and *Sister Love and Other Crime Stories* (Stage 1).

OXFORD BOOKWORMS LIBRARY

Classics • Crime & Mystery • Factfiles • Fantasy & Horror
Human Interest • Playscripts • Thriller & Adventure
True Stories • World Stories

The OXFORD BOOKWORMS LIBRARY provides enjoyable reading in English, with a wide range of classic and modern fiction, non-fiction, and plays. It includes original and adapted texts in seven carefully graded language stages, which take learners from beginner to advanced level. An overview is given on the next pages.

All Stage 1 titles are available as audio recordings, as well as over eighty other titles from Starter to Stage 6. All Starters and many titles at Stages 1 to 4 are specially recommended for younger learners. Every Bookworm is illustrated, and Starters and Factfiles have full-colour illustrations.

The OXFORD BOOKWORMS LIBRARY also offers extensive support. Each book contains an introduction to the story, notes about the author, a glossary, and activities. Additional resources include tests and worksheets, and answers for these and for the activities in the books. There is advice on running a class library, using audio recordings, and the many ways of using Oxford Bookworms in reading programmes. Resource materials are available on the website <www.oup.com/bookworms>.

The *Oxford Bookworms Collection* is a series for advanced learners. It consists of volumes of short stories by well-known authors, both classic and modern. Texts are not abridged or adapted in any way, but carefully selected to be accessible to the advanced student.

You can find details and a full list of titles in the *Oxford Bookworms Library Catalogue* and *Oxford English Language Teaching Catalogues*, and on the website <www.oup.com/bookworms>.

THE OXFORD BOOKWORMS LIBRARY
GRADING AND SAMPLE EXTRACTS

STARTER • 250 HEADWORDS

present simple – present continuous – imperative –
can/cannot, must – *going to* (future) – simple gerunds …

Her phone is ringing – but where is it?

Sally gets out of bed and looks in her bag. No phone. She looks under the bed. No phone. Then she looks behind the door. There is her phone. Sally picks up her phone and answers it. *Sally's Phone*

STAGE 1 • 400 HEADWORDS

… past simple – coordination with *and*, *but*, *or* –
subordination with *before*, *after*, *when*, *because*, *so* …

I knew him in Persia. He was a famous builder and I worked with him there. For a time I was his friend, but not for long. When he came to Paris, I came after him – I wanted to watch him. He was a very clever, very dangerous man. *The Phantom of the Opera*

STAGE 2 • 700 HEADWORDS

… present perfect – *will* (future) – *(don't) have to, must not, could* –
comparison of adjectives – simple *if* clauses – past continuous –
tag questions – *ask/tell* + infinitive …

While I was writing these words in my diary, I decided what to do. I must try to escape. I shall try to get down the wall outside. The window is high above the ground, but I have to try. I shall take some of the gold with me – if I escape, perhaps it will be helpful later. *Dracula*

STAGE 3 • 1000 HEADWORDS

… should, may – present perfect continuous – *used to* – past perfect –
causative – relative clauses – indirect statements …

Of course, it was most important that no one should see
Colin, Mary, or Dickon entering the secret garden. So Colin
gave orders to the gardeners that they must all keep away
from that part of the garden in future. *The Secret Garden*

STAGE 4 • 1400 HEADWORDS

… past perfect continuous – passive (simple forms) –
would conditional clauses – indirect questions –
relatives with *where/when* – gerunds after prepositions/phrases …

I was glad. Now Hyde could not show his face to the world
again. If he did, every honest man in London would be
proud to report him to the police. *Dr Jekyll and Mr Hyde*

STAGE 5 • 1800 HEADWORDS

… future continuous – future perfect –
passive (modals, continuous forms) –
would have conditional clauses – modals + perfect infinitive …

If he had spoken Estella's name, I would have hit him. I was so
angry with him, and so depressed about my future, that I could
not eat the breakfast. Instead I went straight to the old house.
Great Expectations

STAGE 6 • 2500 HEADWORDS

… passive (infinitives, gerunds) – advanced modal meanings –
clauses of concession, condition

When I stepped up to the piano, I was confident. It was as if
I knew that the prodigy side of me really did exist. And when I
started to play, I was so caught up in how lovely I looked that I
didn't worry how I would sound. *The Joy Luck Club*

BOOKWORMS · HUMAN INTEREST · STARTER

Robin Hood

JOHN ESCOTT

'You're a brave man, but I am afraid for you,' says Lady Marian to Robin of Locksley. She is afraid because Robin does not like Prince John's new taxes and wants to do something for the poor people of Nottingham. When Prince John hears this, Robin is suddenly in danger - great danger.

BOOKWORMS · HUMAN INTEREST · STARTER

Star Reporter

JOHN ESCOTT

'There's a new girl in town,' says Joe, and soon Steve is out looking for her. Marietta is easy to find in a small town, but every time he sees her something goes wrong . . . and his day goes from bad to worse.

BOOKWORMS · HUMAN INTEREST · STARTER

The Girl with Red Hair

CHRISTINE LINDOP

Every day people come to Mason's store – old people, young people, men and women. From his office, and in the store, Mark watches them. And when they leave the store, he forgets them. Then one day a girl with red hair comes to the store, and everything changes for Mark. Now he can't forget that beautiful face, those green eyes, and that red hair . . .

BOOKWORMS · CRIME & MYSTERY · STARTER

Give us the Money

MAEVE CLARKE

'Every day is the same. Nothing exciting ever happens to me,' thinks Adam one boring Monday morning. But today is not the same. When he helps a beautiful young woman because some men want to take her bag, life gets exciting and very, very dangerous.

BOOKWORMS · THRILLER & ADVENTURE · STAGE 1

Goodbye, Mr Hollywood

JOHN ESCOTT

Nick Lortz is sitting outside a café in Whistler, a village in the Canadian mountains, when a stranger comes and sits next to him. She's young, pretty, and has a beautiful smile. Nick is happy to sit and talk with her.

But why does she call Nick 'Mr Hollywood'? Why does she give him a big kiss when she leaves? And who is the man at the next table – the man with short white hair?

Nick learns the answers to these questions three long days later – in a police station on Vancouver Island.

BOOKWORMS · CRIME & MYSTERY · STAGE 1

Sister Love and Other Crime Stories

JOHN ESCOTT

Some sisters are good friends, some are not. Sometimes there is more hate in a family than there is love. Karin is beautiful and has lots of men friends, but she can be very unkind to her sister Marcia. Perhaps when they were small, there was love between them, but that was a long time ago.

They say that everybody has one crime in them. Perhaps they only take an umbrella that does not belong to them. Perhaps they steal from a shop, perhaps they get angry and hit someone, perhaps they kill . . .